EXPLORING
ANCIENT INDIA

by Anne E. Johnson

STORY
LIBRARY

12-Story Library is an imprint of Bookstaves and Press Room Editions

Produced for 12-Story Library by Red Line Editorial

Photographs ©: Rattham/iStockphoto, cover, 1; Rainer Lesniewski/Shutterstock Images, 4; hadynyah/iStockphoto, 5; suronin/Shutterstock Images, 6, 7; Studio-Annika/iStockphoto, 8; Los Angeles County Museum of Art (www.lacma.org), 9, 13, 14, 23, 28; Roop_Dey/Shutterstock Images, 10; Kevin Frayer/AP Images, 11; Vladimir Sevrinovsky/Shutterstock Images, 12; reddees/Shutterstock Images, 15; Nila Newsom/Shutterstock Images, 17; Nano Calvo/VWPics/AP Images, 18; Muralinath/iStockphoto, 19; saiko3p/Shutterstock Images, 20; Aleksei Kornev/Shutterstock Images, 21; Cromagnon/Shutterstock Images, 22; Denis Dymov/Shutterstock Images, 24, 29; Casper1774 Studio/Shutterstock Images, 25; Adam68/Shutterstock Images, 26; Nestor Noci/Shutterstock Images, 27

Content Consultant: Namita Sugandhi, Lecturer, Department of Anthropology, Hartwick College

Library of Congress Cataloging-in-Publication Data
Names: Johnson, Anne E., author.
Title: Exploring Ancient India / By Anne E. Johnson.
Description: Mankato, MN : 12 Story Library, 2018. | Series: Exploring
  Ancient Civilizations | Includes bibliographical references and index.
Identifiers: LCCN 2016047640 (print) | LCCN 2016048018 (ebook) | ISBN
  9781632354648 (hardcover : alk. paper) | ISBN 9781632355294 (pbk. : alk.
  paper) | ISBN 9781621435815 (hosted e-book)
Subjects: LCSH: India--Juvenile literature. | India--Social life and
  customs--Juvenile literature. | India--Civilization--Juvenile literature.
Classification: LCC DS407 .J623 2018 (print) | LCC DS407 (ebook) | DDC
  934--dc23
LC record available at https://lccn.loc.gov/2016047640

Printed in the United States of America
022017

Access free, up-to-date content on this topic plus a full digital version of this book. Scan the QR code on page 31 or use your school's login at 12StoryLibrary.com.

Table of Contents

Settlements Sprang Up in the Indus Valley

People have lived in India for thousands of years. India has lots of different environments. It has high mountains, wide valleys, deserts, jungles, rolling hills, and massive rivers.

The land was rich. There was plenty of freshwater. In very early times, people hunted fish, deer, and other animals. They gathered plants for eating and building shelters. Small communities began to grow across northwest India, eastern Pakistan, and northeast Afghanistan. People clustered along the Indus and Ghaggar-Hakra Rivers. People from these communities also traveled south to the Arabian Sea and west to modern Iran. They shared ideas and things with groups living in these places.

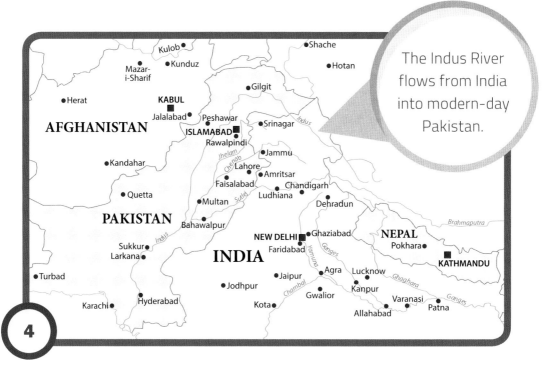

The Indus River flows from India into modern-day Pakistan.

People still farm in the Indus Valley using terraces.

5

Number of rivers that feed into the Indus River.

- People have lived in India for thousands of years.
- They built settlements from eastern Pakistan to the Arabian Sea.
- Settlements grew bigger over time as people farmed and kept livestock.
- By 2600 BCE, people began building cities along the Indus River and in surrounding areas.

Between 8000 and 6000 BCE, some people in India began to farm instead of gather food from the wild. Their diet was nutritious and varied. Farmers grew barley, wheat, and peas. People also grew cotton and wove cloth. Bananas and melons were popular fruits. Sheep and cows provided milk and meat. People even kept cats and dogs as pets.

By 2600 BCE, some of these villages grew into towns. The larger towns became cities. Historians call this the Indus civilization.

The Indus People Built Amazing Cities

Mohenjo Daro and Harappa were two of the biggest cities built by the Indus civilization. The same types of pottery and copper tools were found at both Mohenjo Daro and Harappa. These objects appear at hundreds of other cities, towns, and villages that were part of the Indus civilization, too.

Archaeologists today can see that the cities were planned carefully. Many of these cities and towns had the same basic plan and were surrounded by a wall. Indus cities do not have any large palaces or monuments. Some cities have large brick buildings that may have been used for storage or trading activities.

Archaeologists first visited Mohenjo Daro in 1911.

Harappa was not as well preserved as Mohenjo Daro.

Houses are close together. They were made of brick and had at least two stories. The upper floors looked out over a courtyard. Many houses had their own brick wells.

Nearly everything was made of bricks that were the same size. It takes math and science to make good bricks. The bricks must be heated at the right temperature.

Then they are cut to an even size. The Indus people used them to make streets. Brick sewers ran under the streets. Each house had indoor plumbing. Sewers and sanitation were rare in the ancient world.

ART IN THE INDUS CIVILIZATION

Some of the earliest sculptures in ancient India are small figures of clay called terra-cotta figurines. At Mohenjo Daro, there were terra-cotta figurines of both men and women. Archaeologists have found figurines of cows and many other things. One small stone sculpture of a man found at Mohenjo Daro is known as the "priest-king." However, we do not know who he really was.

Ancient India Was a Center of Trade

The Indus people made a living by trading. They exchanged ideas with the people they met. They brought goods west as far as modern-day Turkey. They sailed across the Arabian Sea to bring goods to the Middle East. They took wood, pearls, and even animals, such as monkeys.

Shallow waters along the coast made India an important source for pearls.

3,500
Number of Indus seals archaeologists have found.

- The Indus people traded goods with people in modern-day Turkey and the Middle East.
- The Indus used seals to label their goods.
- Many Indus seals have images of wild animals.

People in the Indus civilization also used vessels such as this one.

They came home with copper, shells, dates, and incense.

To label their goods, the Indus used seals. The seals are images and symbols carved into soapstone. The seals acted as signatures. The seals made impressions in clay. The clay tags could be tied to a pot or basket. The tag identified who owned the item. Archaeologists believe that different families may have used different images as their seal. But today no one really knows what the seals mean. Common seal images are buffalo, tigers, and other wild animals. Some seals show an animal that looks like a unicorn. Some Indus seals have been found at ancient cities in the Middle East.

4

Climate Change Threatened the Indus Civilization

Archaeologists are not sure what happened to the Indus civilization. Some think changes in nature brought the civilization to an end. Crops and people can die when the climate changes drastically.

Today the Indus River valley is arid. But during the time of the Indus civilization, it was very wet. There may have been monsoon rains. Perhaps it was even a jungle. Indus carvings show animals such as tigers and rhinoceroses. These animals live only in wet climates. Archaeological evidence shows that people built stone dams in the area. Dams are used to hold back water.

Bengal tigers may have lived in the Indus Valley but are now mostly found in India's Sunderbans National Park.

The wet climate in the Indus Valley was good for farmers. They were able to grow rice, wheat, and other crops. But the climate began to change in approximately 2000 BCE. Monsoon rains may have moved to the east. The Indus Valley became drier. Some ancient writings describe the Saraswati River, which was supposedly east of the Indus River. It dried up completely.

The Indus people stopped trading with the Middle East by 1800 BCE. Most of the Indus cities were abandoned. Drought was part of the problem in some regions. There may have been flooding in other areas. There also may have been other social and environmental problems that led to the civilization's end.

The Indus River still floods sometimes, as it did in 2010.

700
Years Mohenjo Daro flourished.

- During the time of the Indus civilization, the climate was very wet.
- By 2000 BCE, the area started to become drier.
- The region became so arid that some rivers may have changed their course or disappeared.
- Foreign trade also stopped during this time.

THINK ABOUT IT

Climate change today is often called global warming. Think about the effects of climate change on the world today. How does climate change today compare to the climate change that happened in the Indus Valley?

New Groups Arrived from Central Asia

Drought and floods changed the Indus Valley. But the Indus people also may have faced other changes. By 1500 BCE, new groups of people who called themselves Aryans began to travel across the Hindu Kush Mountains. They settled in northern India. Historians and archaeologists believe these groups came from Central Asia. Other groups of Aryans traveled into Europe and settled there. Together, these groups are now called Indo-Europeans.

The language they spoke is related to many modern languages in India and Europe. They also have been traced through studies of ancient DNA.

What happened when the Indo-Europeans came to India? Archaeologists and historians do not agree. The Indo-Europeans told stories of fighting battles and conquering other people. But scientists can tell that the Indus civilization was already in decline

The Hindu Kush Mountains are near the border of modern-day Pakistan and Afghanistan.

time, many groups lived by herding cattle and other animals. They moved around from place to place so that their animals would have new grass to eat. This practice is called pastoralism.

This sword was probably made by the Indo-Europeans.

before they arrived. Archaeologists have not found much evidence for violence or warfare. The arrival of these new groups may have been peaceful.

The Indo-Europeans brought with them new ideas and technology. One important item was the chariot. This was a small cart in which one or two people stood. Horses pulled it. Riding a chariot was a fast, easy way to get around. During this

The Indo-Europeans Used Songs to Tell Stories

The Indo-Europeans gathered their religious beliefs into texts called the Vedas. The Vedas include songs, prayers, and ritual instructions. The *Rig Veda* is all their earliest hymns collected together. But it was not just for praying. It told the history of their people and explained how to live a good life.

People believed the god Brahma spoke these teachings to priests. The priests passed the hymns on to the next generation by speaking or singing. The rhythm of their language helped them make up melodies to sing. Some priests sang the melodies. Others repeated long notes called drones on a wind or stringed instrument.

One of *Rig Veda*'s most lasting teachings is the caste system. The caste system organized society. There were four castes. Brahmans were priests. Kshatriyas were

This statue of Brahma was carved approximately 1,000 years after the Indo-Europeans arrived.

10

Number of sections in the *Rig Veda*.

- The *Rig Veda* contains early hymns.
- Ancient Indians believed the god Brahma spoke these teachings to priests.
- Society was separated into four levels, or castes.
- The *Bhagavad-Gita* teaches about duty and living a good life.

THINK ABOUT IT

The caste system was first organized around people's jobs. Later, the caste system became more rigid. Children were born into the same caste as their parents. Go to the library to read more about the Shudra caste. Were Shudra children ever able to move to another caste?

warriors and noblemen. Vaishyas were traders and farmers. Shudras were laborers. There also may have been people who were considered outside of the caste system and treated badly. We do not know exactly how castes were treated in the past, but the caste system creates a lot of injustice in India today.

As time went on, new rules and religious literature were composed. One of the most important works is the *Bhagavad-Gita*. It talks about the importance of living a good life according to duty. The *Bhagavad-Gita* is found

Mahabharata remains a popular topic for art.

in the epic tale *Mahabharata*. This epic includes exciting stories and important lessons of the god Krishna going to war.

Sanskrit Was the Language of Education

The people of the Indus civilization had a special type of writing. They made seals carved with a mixture of pictures and signs. Nobody today knows how to read the Indus script. No translations of the Indus script have survived. Archaeologists do not even agree which spoken language the Indus script represents.

When the Indo-Europeans came to India, they did not bring a system of writing with them. Instead, they brought their language, Sanskrit.

They used Sanskrit for the poetry and stories of the Vedas. The poems all had to be memorized. There was no way to write them down at first.

People in India started creating religious texts around 1200 BCE, but they did not write them down for many more centuries. By 300 BCE, a man named Panini invented a way to standardize written Sanskrit. He also wrote rules for correct Sanskrit grammar. Sanskrit was for educated people and priests.

LANGUAGE IN SOUTH INDIA

Indo-Europeans brought many changes to society in North India, including language. In the southern part of India, people spoke different languages. They are part of the Dravidian language family. People in South India also had their own traditions. Groups in South India and North India traded with one another and shared their ideas. Over time, they began to have more traditions in common. Rulers and priests began to use Sanskrit. But people used their own Dravidian languages as well.

Sanskrit carved into a stone tablet

3,959
Number of grammar rules Panini wrote down for Sanskrit.

- The people of the Indus civilization had a written language that archaeologists do not know how to read.
- The Indo-Europeans in India used languages called Sanskrit and Prakrit.
- Educated people and priests wrote and read Sanskrit.

Sanskrit was used for religious writing, and priests used Panini's rules. Written Sanskrit did not change much over many years. In contrast, the commoner classes spoke a language called Prakrit. Because people spoke Prakrit in everyday life, it kept on changing.

Beliefs in Hinduism Changed Over Time

People in ancient India believed in many gods. In the early poems of the Vedas there was the plant god Soma and the fire god Agni. The warrior god Indra and the wind god Vayu lived above the earth. There were also many other gods and goddesses.

Hinduism changed as time passed. People began to worship different gods. One of those was the god Vishnu. Vishnu helps when things go

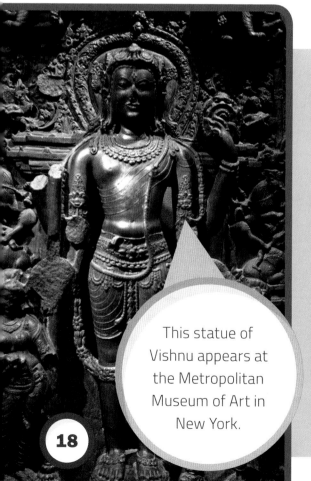

This statue of Vishnu appears at the Metropolitan Museum of Art in New York.

VISHNU AND THE ELIXIR OF IMMORTALITY

In one popular Hindu story, an elixir lay at the bottom of an ocean. It promised immortality. Lakshmi, the goddess of wealth and success, also lay there. Vishnu tricked the demons of the world into helping the gods stir the ocean. After a thousand years, the elixir floated to the top. The gods drank it. They defeated the demons. Lakshmi rose up on a lotus blossom. She made the gods successful forever.

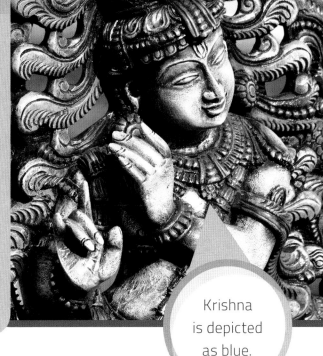

10
Number of incarnations of the god Vishnu.

- Hinduism changed over time.
- There are many different Hindu gods and goddesses.
- Hindus believe Vishnu balances good and evil.
- Vishnu holds a conch shell, a disk, a lotus, and a mace.

Krishna is depicted as blue.

wrong in the world. He brings life back into balance. He chases out evil with good. Hindus also worship Shiva, Lakshmi, and Sarasvati. Ganesha, the elephant-headed god, is worshipped along with many other gods and goddesses.

It is easy to tell when Vishnu is shown in a picture. He has four arms and holds several items. One of those is usually a conch shell. It makes the holy sound *Om* when he blows into it. Another is a chakra, or disk. This shows the importance of the mind. The lotus blossom stands for freedom of the spirit. The mace, a weapon, shows strength.

Hindus believe in reincarnation. This means that the soul of a dead person is reborn in a new person. According to Hindus, we all live multiple lives. Hindus believe a person continues the cycle of birth and rebirth. Eventually, they live a life that is free from any wickedness. Gods are sometimes reincarnated on earth to fight evil. There are many stories about the incarnations of Vishnu. One incarnation of Vishnu was Krishna. His story is told in *Mahabharata*.

Buddhism Was Practiced All Over Ancient India

In approximately 500 BCE, a prince named Siddhartha Gautama gave up all his possessions. He traveled around India teaching. He preached that humans suffer in life because of their attachment to worldly things. He taught that the path to salvation was the Middle Way of good behavior. His followers called him Buddha. This means "The Enlightened One."

Over the next few centuries, Buddhism became popular all over India. One reason for its popularity was its availability to everyone. At the time, Hinduism and knowledge of the Vedas was restricted to upper castes. The growth and spread of Buddhism suggests that people in ancient India may not have been happy with the inequality of the caste system.

Giant sculptures of the Buddha can be found all over India and Asia.

Buddhism is still practiced in India.

As Buddhism spread, its followers began to build monasteries and ceremonial centers where people could study and worship. Important monks were buried in large monuments called stupas. Many Buddhists were involved in trade. Buddhism spread to China and Southeast Asia through trade networks. Buddhism reached China by 100 CE.

2,200
Approximate age, in years, of the Buddhist sanctuary at Sanchi.

- Siddhartha Gautama was Buddha's real name.
- Buddha taught his listeners to follow the Middle Way.
- Buddhism was not restricted to the upper castes of ancient Indian society.
- Buddhism spread to China and Southeast Asia.

THINK ABOUT IT

Both Hinduism and Buddhism were popular religions in ancient India. How are these faiths similar? How are they different?

10

Indo-Greek Kings Ruled the Northwest

Between 800 and 600 BCE, small states formed in North India. Eventually these divided into *mahajanapadas*, independent kingdoms and republics. One of these kingdoms was Gandhara. Its capital city was Taxila. The cities were fortified with walls and moats.

Far to the west, Alexander the Great from Macedon rose to power and conquered Greece. He wanted to conquer the whole world. He conquered the Persian Empire. He reached India sometime around 326 BCE. Alexander fought with the kings in northwest India. The kings' armies had war elephants. The elephants frightened Alexander's cavalry. Alexander conquered some

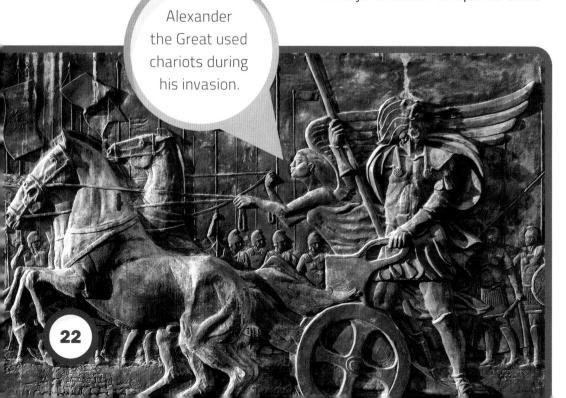

Alexander the Great used chariots during his invasion.

areas anyway. But his army grew tired and refused to continue. Alexander retreated from India. He died in Persia in 323 BCE.

After Alexander's death, his empire was divided up between his generals. The kingdoms in the northwest parts of India were influenced by Greek and Persian culture. We know about many of these Indo-Greek kings from the coins they made. One of the most famous was King Menander. He ruled in the 100s BCE. He was from the Caucasus region between Europe and Asia. Some say he converted to Buddhism.

This coin was made during King Menander's reign.

Ashoka Expands the Mauryan Empire

Magadha was a kingdom in northeastern India. Around 324 BCE, a king named Candragupta Maurya rose to power there. He conquered many surrounding kingdoms in north India. He founded the Mauryan Empire.

Candragupta Maurya had a grandson named Ashoka. Ashoka became emperor in 268 BCE. He fought a few extremely bloody and brutal wars. But stories about him say he grew tired of fighting. He stopped expanding his empire. He tried to focus on making life better for the people of India.

Ashoka ordered the construction of the Buddhist Mahabodhi temple.

38
Number of years Ashoka was emperor of India.

- Candragupta Maurya was the first emperor of the Mauryan Empire.
- Ashoka expanded the empire but later gave up wars and fighting.
- Ashoka was Buddhist and helped spread the religion.

A pillar carved with Ashoka's edicts

ASHOKA'S EDICTS

We do not know how much of India was controlled by the Mauryan Empire under Ashoka. He set up inscriptions that are found everywhere in India. On these inscriptions, his scribes carved the emperor's words. There are lists of things the emperor did. The lists also include things he wanted to do. All of the items, or edicts, have to do with making people's lives better. One edict describes how he planted trees. Another describes how he dug wells and built places for people to rest.

Perhaps the most important thing about Ashoka was his Buddhist faith. His beliefs helped him make decisions about ruling. There are many stories about the way he supported Buddhism. During his reign, Buddhism grew from a small following to a major religion. According to one ancient story, Ashoka built 84,000 Buddhist stupas.

25

The Gupta Empire Ushered in a Classical Age

After the Mauryan Empire, many other smaller kingdoms rose and fell in India. South India had several kingdoms, such as the Satavahanas and Cholas. A new dynasty came to power in North India in 320 CE. Chandra Gupta I became a ruler in the Magadha region. Then he married a princess. Her family controlled a large part of northeastern India. He conquered many surrounding kingdoms, too. His lands became known as the Gupta Empire.

Chandra Gupta's son, Samudra Gupta, expanded the empire even farther. He conquered many territories across northern India. He fought against kings and added their lands to the Gupta Empire. But Samudra Gupta was not a harsh ruler. He accepted many religions. He supported the arts. He was a poet and musician as well as a warrior.

Many historians believe the Gupta rulers ushered in a classical age in Indian history. Gupta emperors

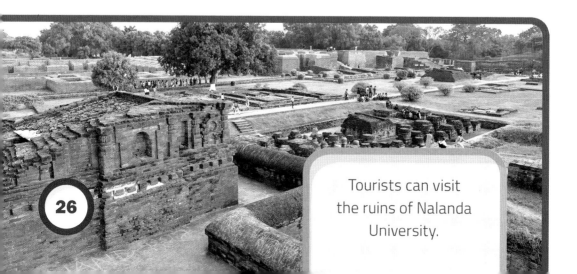

Tourists can visit the ruins of Nalanda University.

Trees and other plants hid the Ajanta Caves from view for hundreds of years.

THE AJANTA CAVES

Some of the oldest Buddhist artwork can be found in the Ajanta Caves in western India. The caves are Buddhist temples and monasteries that were carved into a cliff. Many of the mural paintings inside the caves were added during India's classical age. The caves were abandoned in approximately 500 CE. They were forgotten for centuries. A British officer rediscovered them in 1819. The caves are now a popular tourist attraction.

embraced art, science, and religion. Playwrights and poets produced many works. Other writers penned essays about medicine, math, or astronomy. Later Gupta emperors founded Nalanda University in northeast India. It was a center of Buddhist learning.

The Gupta Empire eventually fell to the Huns from northern China. The empire disappeared completely by 550 CE. But India's classical age was not forgotten.

50

Number of years Samudra Gupta was emperor.

- Chandra Gupta I was a ruler in the Magadha kingdom.
- Samudra Gupta expanded the Gupta Empire.
- Gupta emperors supported the arts, science, and religion.
- The Gupta period is known as India's classical age.

12 Key Dates

6000 BCE
People establish farming settlements in the Indus Valley.

2600 BCE
The Indus people begin building cities.

1800 BCE
Drought and flooding affect many Indus cities.

1500 BCE
Indo-European groups travel across the Hindu Kush Mountains into India.

500 BCE
Siddhartha Gautama, more commonly known as Buddha, gives up his possessions.

400–200 BCE
The Indian epic *Mahabharata* is written.

326 BCE
Alexander the Great retreats from India.

324 BCE
Candragupta Maurya comes to power and begins the Mauryan Empire.

300 BCE
Panini writes down the formal grammar rules for Sanskrit.

268–232 BCE
Ashoka rules the Mauryan Empire.

320 CE
The Gupta Empire begins to rule in India and begins a classical age.

550 CE
The Gupta Empire falls to the Huns.

Glossary

dynasty
A series of rulers who belong to the same family.

epic
A long story or poem about heroic adventures.

hymns
A song of praise to a god.

incarnations
Physical forms, such as animals, in which a Hindu god can appear.

monasteries
Buildings where monks live and work.

monks
Men who live in religious communities and devote their lives to their religion.

monsoon
A time of very heavy rainfall.

reincarnation
When the soul of a dead person comes back in a new person.

sanitation
The process of keeping places free from dirt and disease.

For More Information

Books

Ali, Daud. *Ancient India*. New York: Rosen Publishing, 2009.

Hynson, Colin. *Understanding Indian Myths*. New York: Crabtree Publishing, 2013.

Roxburgh, Ellis. *The Mauryan Empire of India*. New York: Cavendish Square Publishing, 2016.

Wood, Alix. *Uncovering the Culture of Ancient India*. New York: PowerKids Press, 2016.

Visit 12StoryLibrary.com

Scan the code or use your school's login at **12StoryLibrary.com** for recent updates about this topic and a full digital version of this book. Enjoy free access to:

- Digital ebook
- Breaking news updates
- Live content feeds
- Videos, interactive maps, and graphics
- Additional web resources

Note to educators: Visit 12StoryLibrary.com/register to sign up for free premium website access. Enjoy live content plus a full digital version of every 12-Story Library book you own for every student at your school.

Index

About the Author

Anne E. Johnson is a freelance writer who has written many fiction and nonfiction books for kids. She currently lives in Brooklyn, New York.